HANDEL

O praise the Lord with one consent

NINTH CHANDOS ANTHEM

for soprano, alto, tenor & bass soli, SATB & orchestra

piano accompaniment from the score with additional
accompaniments by Edouard Silas

Order No: NOV 070141

NOVELLO PUBLISHING LIMITED
8/9 Frith Street, London W1V 5TZ

O PRAISE THE LORD WITH ONE CONSENT.

No. 1. CHORUS.—"O PRAISE THE LORD WITH ONE CONSENT." G. F. HANDEL.

3

and mag-ni - fy, ... and mag-ni - fy His Name.

. . . . and mag-ni - fy, and mag-ni - fy His Name.

Name, ... and mag - ni - fy His Name.

- fy, ... and mag-ni - fy His Name.

Let all the ser - vants of the Lord His

Let all the

L.H.

wor - - thy praise, His worthy praise proclaim,

servants of the Lord His worthy praise proclaim, let all the servants of the

Let all the servants of the Lord, let all the servants of the

No. 2.   AIR.--"PRAISE HIM, ALL YE THAT IN HIS HOUSE ATTEND.

No. 8. Air.—"FOR THIS OUR TRUEST INT'REST."

glad hymns of praise, . . . of praise to sing,

glad hymns of praise, ... glad hymns of praise to sing,

and with loud songs to bless His Name,

and with loud songs . . to bless His Name, a most de - light - ful

No. 4.

SOLO.—"THAT GOD IS GREAT.

God .. is great . . . .

. . . . we of - en

have by glad ex - pe - rience found, by glad ex - pe-rience,

by glad ex - pe - - - - - - - - - - -

- - - - . . . - - - - - rience,

23

a - bove all gods . . . . . . is crown'd, and seen how He, with won - drous pow'r, a - bove all gods, ... a - bove all gods is crown'd, a - bove all gods, a - bove all gods is crown'd.

No. 5.   CHORUS.—"WITH CHEERFUL NOTES LET ALL THE EARTH."

to heaven their voic - es raise.

to heaven their voic - es raise.

to heaven their voic - es raise.

to heaven their voic - es raise.

31

33

8107.

No. 6.   Solo.—"GOD'S TENDER MERCY KNOWS NO BOUNDS."

shall ne'er de - - cay, God's ten-der mer - cy knows no bounds, His truth . . . shall ne'er . . . de - cay, His truth shall ne'er de - - cay, then let . . . the will - ing na - tions round Their grate - - ful tri - bute

joy, ex - alt your Maker's fame, ex - alt your Ma - ker's fame,

- alt your Maker's fame, ex - alt your Ma - ker's fame,

joy, ex - alt your Maker's fame, ex - alt your Ma - ker's fame,

fame, ex - alt your Ma - ker's fame, ex - alt your Ma - ker's fame,

His praise your song em-ploy,

His praise your song em - ploy,

His praise your song em - ploy, His praise your song employ A-bove the

His praise your song em - ploy,

His praise your song employ A-bove the star - ry frame, . .

His praise your song employ A-bove the star - ry frame, a-bove the

star - ry . . frame, ... His

His praise your song employ A-bove the star - ry frame, His

42

8107.

44

8107.

Chorus.—"YOUR VOICES RAISE."

49

8107.

Se - ra-phin, ye Che - ru-bin and
. . . . ye Che - ru - bin and Se - ra-phin,
Se - ra-phin, ye Che - ru-bin and
ye Che - ru - bin and Se - ra-phin,
Se - ra-phin, to sing His praise, Al - le - lu - ja, Al -
to sing His praise, Al - le - lu - ja, Al -
Se - ra-phin, to sing His praise, Al - le - lu - ja, Al -
to sing His praise, Al - le - lu - ja, ...
- le - lu - ja, Al-le-lu-ja, Al - le - lu - - ja, Al-le-lu-ja, ...
- le - lu - ja, Al-le-lu-ja, ... Al - le - lu - ja, ...
- le - lu - ja, Al-le-lu-ja, Al - le - lu - - ja, Al-le-lu-ja, Al-le-lu -
. . . . . Al - le - lu - ja, . . .

Printed and bound in Great Britain by
Caligraving Limited Thetford Norfolk

THE END.

9/08(166811)